SHAKESPEARE'S MONOLOGUES
THEY HAVEN'T HEARD

Edited by Dick Dotterer

Dramaline Publications

Dramaline Publications
36851 Palm View Road
Rancho Mirage, CA 92270
Phone 619/770-6076 Fax 619/770-4507

Cover art, Teri Karshner

This book is printed on 55# Glatfelter acid-free paper. A paper that meets the requirements of the American Standard of Permanence of paper for printed library material.

CONTENTS

DEDICATION

To most of the actors and students with whom I have worked, and to many of them with whom I wish to work again, but especially for Tony, Carey, Joe, Gary, Marnie, Cheri, Dorothy, and, of course, Victoria and Bill.

PREFACE TO THE SECOND EDITION

Over the years I have been witness to numerous auditions. These have included auditions by students for scholarships and/or placement in a school's theatre program; for places in seasonal resident companies; for acceptance into membership theatre companies; and for individual productions. I have also auditioned in many of these circumstances.

In most situations in which an actor is required to present a "classical" piece, I am struck by one recurring fact: the actor seems to choose material only from a few well-known pieces. Actors appear to be limited in their knowledge of what is available. I have had to listen to the same old war-horses again and again, pieces the actor learned at the knee of a junior high school English teacher, I am sure. I have wondered, at times, if there is a law of which I am unawares which mandates that actors can only do certain pieces.

The choices the actors made were not in themselves bad. (More than one actor did insist, however, on doing a piece only because it was familiar, without regard as to whether it was personally suitable or not. The actor seemed not to want to dig a little deeper into the literature and often the chosen material was damaging.) Some of the choices were so familiar that we could, without hesitation, cue the floundering actor, and we knew instantly, too, if anything was being omitted from the pieces.

Although to do a familiar well-known piece for an audition is not a mistake, many times it's more of a miscalculated risk than is supposed. If an actor does material that is overly exposed or very familiar to the auditors, several things need to be considered (not the least of which is the suitability of the material for the actor's purposes).

If an actor chooses material that is well-known, he runs the risk that the auditor may (1) be tired or bored-to-distraction with that particular piece; (2) once the familiar piece begins, the auditor may automatically tune in to certain expectations: his ear may be set to hear the piece done one particular way and he may object if it is done otherwise; and (3) the auditor may, consciously or unconsciously, compare the actors to others, in the audition or, perhaps, from other performances—and his comparison can often be detrimental to the actor's chances.

There is always some risk in selecting material for an audition: it is part of the adventure of being an actor, and part of the fun. But if an actor is astute, anticipating some of the calculated advantages of doing material that is not frequently heard will be most beneficial.

Unfamiliar material catches the auditor's interest: something *new* is being done! something that hasn't been heard before! something to listen to with revitalized attention! The actor can also make a memorable impact on the auditor by his choice of material. In a long day of auditions, the unique actor always gets the asterisk beside his name. And, finally, when it comes to the inevitable comparison with other actors, the audacious actor knows that the comparison is between apples and persimmons, and not just among apples.

Shakespeare's plays are caskets of jewels of singular audition and/or scene-study pieces. There are sparkling stones in the middle and the bottom of the boxes as well as the glittering light catchers at the top. This book contains twenty-eight such uncovered jewels from eighteen of Shakespeare's plays. They are identified as either humorous or serious in intent; for either young women or young men; mature women or mature men. And while many of the pieces mark an age, many also specify that they can be done by any age—such is the universality of Shakespeare's situations. There are selections in both Shakespearean prose and verse. They are categorized, too, by one of the four accepted labels for the playscripts: the Comedies, the Romances, the Histories, and the Tragedies.

This book is meant to be, above all, a resource of material for the active, concentrated actor. This book should be thought of as a tool in the study of acting, Shakespeare, and blank verse. [There is much to learn in handling blank verse. Blank verse is something that is not recited in sing-song, nor is it by its very nature "naturalistic" everyday speech. It is a conscious style and requires a technique all of its own. The way it is formed in the speeches gives clues as to how it should be delivered.]

And even though I have tried to give the actor something from which to build a characterization in each of the introductions, it should be self-evident that to do the pieces and the characters justice, the actor should take time to read, and even to study, the playscript from which the piece comes. The actor will then know exactly where the specific piece falls within the dramatic action's build of the play and its relevancy to the play as a whole.

The selections in this book were chosen to give the actor a multiplicity of material, so that he could return to this book again and again as a prime source of material for workshops and/or auditions. This book should be thought of as a scene-study book as much as a quick source for "classic" audition material. These pieces have been consciously edited so that each one represents a short scene, each with something for the actor to *act*. And since the pieces vary in length, they should also be considered pliable: the actor should feel free to adapt the speeches to the durations that suit his needs.

For most, these Shakespearean mono-scenes will be a new experience. To some others, they may even be newly discovered treasures. Most of all, I hope, the actor will find them a pleasure to do.

Finally, to whomever uses this book, I wish you the best of success in whatever your endeavors.

DICK DOTTERER

THE COMEDIES

THE COMEDY of ERRORS
LUCIANA—ACT III, SCENE 2

AGE: Young. INTENT: Humorous

Mistaken identity was a stock-in-trade with Shakespeare, and he became enamored with this device early in his career. *The Comedy of Errors* contains not one, but *two* sets of identical twins to confuse the citizens of Ephesus. And neither set of twins knows about his other half—that he is a twin. One set, the masters, are known as Antipholus of Ephesus and Antipholus of Syracuse. Their servants (the other set of identical twins) are Dromio of Ephesus and Dromio of Syracuse. Antipholus is married to Adriana; Antipholus of Syracuse is a bachelor. Soon after his arrival in Ephesus, Antipholus of Syracuse meets Luciana, who happens to be Adriana's sister. Antipholus of Syracuse is smitten with Luciana and pursues her with vigor and intent. Luciana, however, doesn't know there are *two* Antipholuses: she assumes that the one chasing her is her brother-in-law. And on this gossamer hinge swings the fun.

LUCIANA

And may it be that you have quite forgot
    A husband's office? shall Antipholus,
Even in the spring of love, thy love-springs rot?
    Shall love, in building, grow so ruinous?
If you did wed my sister for her wealth,
    Then for her wealth's sake use her with more kindness;
Or if you like elsewhere, do it by stealth:
    Muffle your false love with some show of blindness.
Let not my sister read it in your eye;
    Be not thy tongue thy own shame's orator;
Look sweet, speak fair, become disloyalty;
    Apparel vice like virtue's harbinger;
Bear a fair presence, though your heart be tainted;
    Teach sin the carriage of a holy saint;

Be secret-false: what need she be acquainted?
    What simple thief brags of his own attaint?
'Tis double wrong, to truant with your bed
    And let her read it in thy looks at board:
Shame hath a bastard fame, well managed;
    Ill deeds are doubled with an evil word.
Alas, poor women! make us but believe,
    Being compact of credit, that you love us;
Though others have the arm, show us the sleeve;
    We in your motion turn and you may move us.
Then, gentle brother, get you in again;
    Comfort my sister, cheer her, call her wife:
'Tis holy sport to be a little vain
    When the sweet breath of flattery conquers strife.

LOVE'S LABOUR'S LOST
BOYET—ACT V, SCENE 2

AGE: Mature [Any age]   INTENT: Humorous

*L*ove's Labour's Lost is a courtly play. The King of Navarre and his court of young lords have forsworn the company of women and all others for a period of three years to devote themselves to study and more "aesthetic" pursuits. Shortly after they have signed their oaths, however, the Princess of France and her court of young ladies arrive in the district for a visit. Very soon, young men meet young ladies, and the courtship begins.

Boyet is a lord attached to the French Princess's entourage. He is much like her chaperon, and he is there under the directive of the French king. He is a tutor, father-confessor, bon-vivant, and surrogate father-figure to the French Princess and her ladies.

While the King of Navarre and his attending young lords were in the field plotting their escapades to court the young French ladies, Boyet was, quite by dramatic coincidence, trying to take a nap under a near-by tree and convenient bushes. The ruckus of the young lords wakes him and he spies on them, learning of their plans to come "in disguise" and "to test" the loyalty of the ladies. Not only is it his duty, it is also his delight to come to the Princess and her ladies and tell them his tale.

BOYET

Prepare, madam, prepare!
Arm, wenches, arm! encounters mounted are
Against your peace: Love doth approach disguised,
Armed in arguments; you'll be surprised:
Muster your wits; stand in your own defence;
Or hide your heads like cowards, and fly hence.
Under the cool shade of a sycamore
I thought to close mine eyes some half an hour,
When, lo! to interrupt my purpos'd rest,
Toward that shade I might behold addrest
The king and his companions: warily
I stole into the neighbour thicket by,
And over heard what you shall overhear:
That, by and by, disguis'd they will be here.
Their herald is a pretty knavish page,
That well by heart hath conn'd his embassage:
Action and accent did they teach him there:
'Thus must thou speak,' and 'thus thy body bear';
And ever and anon they made a doubt
Presence majestical would put him out;
'For,' quoth the king, 'an angel shalt thou see;
Yet fear not thou, but speak audaciously.'
The boy replied, 'An angel is not evil;
I should have feared her had she been a devil.'
With that, all laugh'd and clapp'd him on the shoulder,
Making the bold wag by their praises bolder.
One rubb'd his elbow thus, and fleer'd, and swore
A better speech was never spoke before;
Another, with his finger and his thumb,
Cried, 'Via! we will do't, come what will come';
The third he caper'd, and cried, 'All goes well';
The fourth turn'd on the toe, and down he fell.
With that, they all did tumble on the ground,

With such a zealous laughter, so profound,
That in this spleen ridiculous appears,
To check their folly, passion's solemn tears.
They come, they come; and apparell'd thus,
Like Muscovites, or Russians, as I guess.
Their purpose is to parle, to court and dance;
And every one his love-feat will advance
Unto his several mistress, which they'll know
By favours several which they did bestow.
          [*Trumpets sound within.*]
The trumpet sounds: be mask'd; the maskers come.

THE MERCHANT of VENICE
LAUNCELOT GOBBO—ACT II, SCENE 2

AGE: Young [any age]   INTENT: Humorous

Launcelot Gobbo is the designated "clown" role in *The Merchant of Venice*. He is a servant of the Jewish usurer, Shylock. Lanucelot feels that Shylock has "done me wrong," and he wishes to leave the Jew. To leave employment, however, without a promised position to go to is a very dangerous thing to contemplate: one risks becoming a vagrant by not finding employment; and a vagrant is a criminal by current laws. Launcelot soon solicits—and receives—employment from Bassanio, a young man who wishes to win Portia, the rich heiress at Belmont, to wife.

This monologue is the first speech and the first time an audience meets Launcelot Gobbo in the story. He is walking along the street in Venice, arguing with himself as to whether he should leave the service of Shylock or not—and how he can justify his actions.

LAUNCELOT GOBBO

Certainly my conscience will serve me to run from this Jew my master. The fiend is at mine elbow and tempts me saying to me 'Gobbo, Launcelot Gobbo, good Launcelot,' or 'good Gobbo,' or 'good Launcelot Gobbo, use you legs, take the start, run away.' My conscience says 'No; take heed honest Launcelot; take heed, honest Gobbo,' or, as aforesaid, ' honest Launcelot Gobbo; do not run; scorn running with thy heels.' Well, the most courageous fiend bids me pack: 'Viva!' says the fiend; 'away!' says the fiend: 'for the heavens, rouse up a brave mind,' says the fiend 'and run.' Well, my conscience, hanging about the neck of my heart, says very wisely to me 'My honest friend Launcelot, being an honest man's son,' or rather an honest woman's son; for, indeed, my father did something smack, something grow to, he had a kind of taste; well, my conscience says 'Launcelot, budge not.' 'Budge,' says the fiend. 'Budge not,' says my conscience. 'Conscience,' I say, 'you counsel well;' 'Fiend,' say I, ' you counsel well:' to be ruled by my conscience, I should stay with the Jew my master, who, God bless the mark, is a kind of devil; and, to run away from the Jew, I should be ruled by the fiend, who saving your reverence, is the devil himself. Certainly the Jew is the very devil incarnal; and, in my conscience, my conscience is but a kind of hard conscience, to offer to counsel me to stay with the Jew. The fiend gives the more friendly counsel: I will run, fiend; my heels are at your command; I will run.

THE MERCHANT of VENICE
PORTIA—ACT III, SCENE 2

AGE: Young   INTENT: Serious

Portia has been left an enormous fortune, which makes her one of the most desirable marriage prospects in Europe. But her late, far-seeing father knew that because of the estate Portia would be pursued by avaricious suitors of all sorts. To make sure that she did not choose wrongly, or that the wrong choice did not win her, Portia's father left provisions that she must be won in a contest: the prospective groom must choose among a gold, silver, and a lead casket. In one of them is a portrait of Portia. The suitor who finds the portrait wins both Portia and the fortune. However, if the suitor chooses wrong, he looses Portia, the fortune, and he must swear never to seek any other lady in marriage for the rest of his life.

Portia has had a number of suitors, all of whom have chosen wrongly, and all of whom she has not regretted to see go or pitied their fate. But into her world at Belmont comes the young Venetian, Bassanio, and she does not want to lose his company. Bassanio, impatient and anxious as youth is inclined to be, wants to chance his luck with the caskets without delay.

PORTIA

I pray you, tarry: a day or two
Before you hazard; for, in choosing wrong,
I lose your company: therefore forbear awhile.
There's something tells me, but it is not love,
I would not lose you; and you know yourself,
Hate counsels not in such quality.
But lest you should not understand me well,—
And yet a maiden hath no tongue but thought,—
I would detain you here some month or two
Before you venture for me. I could teach you
How to choose right, but I am then forsworn;
So will I never be: so may you miss me;
But if you do, you'll make me wish a sin,
That I had been forsworn. Beshrew your eyes,
They have o'er look'd me and divided me;
One half of me is yours, the other half yours,
Mine own, I would say; but if mine, then yours,
And so all yours. O, these naughty times
Put bars between the owners and their rights!
And so, though yours, not yours. Prove it so,
Let fortune go to hell for it, not I.
I speak too long; but 'tis to peize the time,
To eke it and to draw it out in length,
To stay you from election.
Away, then! I am lock'd in one of them:
If you do love me, you will find me out.
Nerissa and the rest, stand all aloof.
Let music sound while he doth make his choice;
Then, if he lose, he makes a swan-like end,

Fading in music: that the comparison
May stand more proper, my eye shall be the stream
And watery death-bed for him. He may win;
And what is music then? The music is
Even as the flourish when true subjects bow
To the new-crowned monarch: such it is
As are those dulcet sounds in break of day
That creep into the dreaming bridegroom's ear
And summon him to marriage. Now he goes,
With no less presence, but with much more love,
Than young Alcides, when he did redeem
The virgin tribute paid by howling Troy
To the sea-monster: I stand for sacrifice;
The rest aloof are the Dardanian wives,
With bleared visages, come forth to view
The issue of the exploit. Go, Hercules!
Live thou, I live: with much much more dismay
I view the fight than thou that makest the fray.

THE MERRY WIVES of WINDSOR
MISTRESS PAGE—ACT II, SCENE 1

AGE: Mature [Any age]   INTENT: Humorous

*T*he *Merry Wives of Windsor*, the third of the "Falstaff plays," is the only play Shakespeare wrote which he centered in his own middle class. Sir John Falstaff, the fat knight of inflated fame, frame, and little fortune, pictures himself as much the lady's man—yea, a lady-killer —a man that no woman can resist. He is, of course, an old reprobate and easy to reject. At present Sir John has *two* objects de couer" in the township of Windsor, both married women: Mistress Page and Mistress Ford. Falstaff has written identical letters to each woman. Rather than be flattered by Sir John's protestations of love to each of them, both women are irritated by his effrontery.

Mistress Page has just received Sir John's letter, and she is reading it for the first time.

MISTRESS PAGE

What, have I scaped love-letters in the holiday-time of my beauty, and am I now a subject for them? Let me see. [*Reads.*]

'Ask me no reason why I love you; for though Love use Reason for his physician, he admits him not for his counsellor. You are not young, no more than I am; go to then, there's sympathy: you are merry, so am I; ha, ha! then there's more sympathy: you love sack, and so do I; would you desire better sympathy? Let it suffice thee, Mistress Page,—at the least, if the love of a soldier can suffice,—that I love thee. I will not say, pity me; 'tis not a soldier-like phrase: but I say, love me. By me,

> Thine own true knight,
> By day or night,
> Or any kind of light,
> With all his might
> For thee to fight,
> John Falstaff.'

What a Herod of Jewry is this! O wicked, wicked world! One that is well-nigh worn to pieces with age to show himself a young gallant! What an unweighed behavior hath this Flemish Drunkard picked—with the devil's name!—out of my conversation, that he dares in this manner assay me? Why, he hath not been thrice in my company! What should I say to him? I was then frugal of my mirth: Heaven forgive me! Why, I'll exhibit a bill in the parliament for the putting down of men. How shall I be revenged on him? for revenged I will be, as sure as his guts are made of puddings.

THE MERRY WIVES of WINDSOR
MASTER FORD—ACT II, SCENE 2

AGE: Mature [Any age.]   INTENT: Humorous

Both Master Ford and Master Page know of the outrageous behavior Sir John Falstaff has exhibited toward each of their wives with his letter writing to them. Master Page, however, has confidence in his wife and her virtue, so he is not threatened by the situation. Master Ford, on the other hand, is a jealous man. Ford disguises himself and assumes the name of "Master Brook" to meet Falstaff at a local tavern, the Garter Inn.

As Brook, Ford offers Falstaff money to "woo" Mistress Ford in his behalf. He wishes Falstaff "to win" the lady, and then he (Ford as Brook) will use the evidence of her liaison with Falstaff to "tear down Mistress Ford's resistance" and be able to bed her himself, as he professes he wants so much to do. Falstaff, with an ego of delusions that knows no bounds, says the deed will be accomplished between ten and eleven that very night.

MASTER FORD

What damned Epicurean rascal is this! My heart is ready to crack with impatience. Who says this is improvident jealousy? my wife hath sent him; the hour is fixed; the match is made. Would any man have thought this? See the hell of having a false woman! My bed shall be abused, my coffers ransacked, my reputation gnawn at; and I shall not only receive this villanous wrong, but stand under the adoption of abominable terms, and by him that does me this wrong. Terms! names! Amaimon sounds well; Lucifer, well; Barbason, well; yet they are devils' additions, the names of fiends; but Cuckold! Wittol!— Cuckold! the devil himself hath not such a name. Page is an ass, a secure ass: he will trust his wife; he will not be jealous. I will rather trust a Fleming with my butter, Parson Hugh the Welshman with my cheese, an Irishman with my aqua-vitae bottle, or a thief to walk my ambling gelding, than my wife with herself: then she plots, then she ruminates, then she devises; and what they think in their hearts they may effect, they will break their hearts but they will effect. God be praised for my jealously! Eleven o'clock the hour. I will prevent this, detect my wife, be revenged on Falstaff, and laugh at Page. I will about it; better three hours too soon than a minute too late. Fie, fie, fie! cuckold! cuckold! cuckold.

THE ROMANCES

MEASURE for MEASURE
DUKE VINCENTIO—ACT III, SCENE 1

AGE: Mature   INTENT: Serious

Measure for Measure is about governments, governing, and government officials. Duke Vincentio wants to see first hand, and unnoticed, the working of justice in his realm. To that end, he "retires" for a time in retreat, assigning his powers and duties to his deputy, Lord Angelo. Angelo is a hard and puritanical man. One of Angelo's first official decrees is to condemn Claudio to death for sleeping with a woman he is unable to marry. The only way for Claudio to be reprieved is for his sister, Isabella, a novice nun, to sleep with Angelo. Isabella refuses to comply, saying she would rather lose her body than her soul. The Duke has been aware of these actions as an observer. He has been roaming Vienna disguised as a friar, and it is in this disguise that the Duke visits the city prisons. There, he encounters Claudio, who waits in "hope" for a pardon from Angelo. But Claudio also tells the unknown "friar," with little conviction that he is also "prepared to die."

DUKE VINCENTIO

So then you hope for a pardon from Lord Angelo?
Be absolute for death; either death or life
Shall thereby be sweeter. Reason thus with life:
If I do lose thee, I do lose a thing
That none but fools would keep: a breath thou art,
Servile to all the skyey influences
That dost this habitation, where thou keep'st,
Hourly afflict: merely, thou art death's fool;
For him thou labour'st by thy flight to shun
And yet runn'st toward him still. Thou art not noble;
For all the accommodations that thou bear'st
Are nursed by baseness. Thou'rt by no means valiant;
For thou dost fear the soft and tender fork

Of a poor worm. Thy best of rest is sleep,
And that thou oft provokest; yet grossly fear'st
Thy death, which is no more. Thou art not thyself;
For thou exist'st on many a thousand grains
That issue out of dust. Happy thou art not;
For what thou has not, still thou strivest to get,
And what thou hast, forget'st. Thou art not certain;
For thy complexion shifts to strange effects,
After the moon. If thou art rich, thou 'rt poor;
For, like an ass whose back with ingots bows,
Thou bear'st thy heavy riches but a journey,
And death unloads thee. Friend hast thou none;
For thine own bowels, which do call thee sire,
The mere effusion of thy proper loins,
Do curse the gout, serpigo, and the rheum,
For ending thee no sooner. Thou hast nor youth nor age,
But, as it were, an after-dinner's sleep,
Dreaming on both; for all thy blessed youth
Becomes as aged, and doth beg the alms
Of palsied eld; and when thou art old and rich,
Thou hast neither heat, affection, limb, nor beauty,
To make thy riches pleasant. What's yet in this
That bears the name of life? Yet in this life
Lie hid moe thousand deaths: yet death we fear,
That makes these odds all even.

PERICLES
PERICLES—ACT I, SCENE 2

AGE: Young   INTENT: Serious

This is an extraordinary adventure play and an extraordinarily experimental one. *Pericles* is a "phantastic" play, and one that was extremely popular and successful in Shakespeare's theatre. Pericles' adventures are, however, painful ones, and that is one of the things that gave it its appeal.

Pericles, Prince of Tyre, goes to the court of King Antiochus in Antioch to court the king's daughter in marriage. Pericles, however, guesses the secret incest between the king and daughter and has to flee for his life.

Pericles has returned from Antioch to his home in Tyre. He is still shaken by the discovery of the incest between the powerful King Antiochus and his daughter. To keep the guilty secret, Antiochus has killed all other suitors. Pericles escaped. He has not, up to this point, told anyone of his discoveries in Antioch. One of the prince's trusted lords, Helicanus, has badgered Pericles into confession. At last, like a man who needs to voice his thoughts or explode, Here Pericles relates his tale.

PERICLES

Thou speak'st like a physician, Helicanus,
That minister'st a potion unto me
That thou wouldst tremble to receive thyself.
Attend me, then: I went to Antioch
Where as thou know'st, against the face of death,
I sought the purchase of a glorious beauty,
From whence an issue I might propagate,
Are arms to princes, and brings joys to subjects.
Her face was to mine eye beyond all wonder;
The rest—hark in thine ear—as black as incest:
Which by my knowledge found, the sinful father
Seem'd not to strike, but smooth: but thou know'st this,
'Tis time to fear when tyrants seem to kiss.
Which fear so grew in me, I hither fled,
Under the covering of a careful night,
Who seem'd my good protector; and, being here,
Bethought me what was past, what might succeed.
I knew him tyrannous; and tyrants' fears
Decrease not, but grow faster than the years:
And should he doubt it, as no doubt he doth,
That I should open to the listening air
How many worthy princes' bloods were shed,
To keep his bed of blackness unlaid ope,

To lop that doubt, he'll fill this land with arms,
And make pretence of wrong that I have done him;
When all, for mine, if I may call offence,
Must feel war's blow, who spares not innocence:
Which love to all, of which thyself art one,
Who now reprovest me for it—
Drew sleep out of mine eyes, blood from my cheeks,
Musing into my mind, with thousand doubts
How I might stop this tempest ere it came;
And finding little comfort to relieve them,
I thought it princely charity to grieve them.
Tyre, I now look from thee then, and to Tarsus
Intend my travel, where I'll hear from thee;
And by whose letters I'll dispose myself.
The care I had and have of subjects' good
On thee I lay, whose wisdom's stength can bear it.
I'll take thy word for faith, not ask thine oath:
Who shuns not to break one will sure crack both:
But in our orbs we'll live round and safe,
That time of both this truth shall ne'er convince
Thou show'dst a subject's shine, I a true prince.

CYMBELINE
IMOGEN—ACT IV, SCENE 2

AGE: Young   INTENT: Serious

*C*ymbeline must have come as a surprise to Shakespeare's
audiences of Jacobean England. They knew Shakespeare as a
writer of comedies, tragedies, and histories. Then comes *Cymbeline*.

It is a curious play, an experimental one. It leans toward romance;
it has a fairy-tale background; and its principle plot is rooted in folk-
lore's love-wager theme. Shakespeare might have written it with his
quill planted firmly in his cheek; or he might have considered it a
serious attempt to produce a "tragi-comedy." The play was greatly
admired in the 19th century, and the heroine, Imogen, was one of the
most admired ladies in Shakespeare's canon. She was regarded as a

combination of the magnanimity, forebearance, and fortitude of Hermione (*The Winter's Tale*) and the gentleness and grace of Desdemona (*Othello*).

Imogen is the daughter of Cymbeline, king of ancient Britain. She is secretly married to a "poor but worthy gentleman," Posthumus Leonatus. When the marriage is revealed, Cymbeline objects and exiles Posthumus. Through a set of circumstances to complicated to detail here, Posthumus believes Imogen is unfaithful to him, though she isn't. He orders his servant to kill her, which the servant doesn't. Instead, Imogen escapes in male disguise. She becomes servant to Belarius and his two "sons," who just happen to be her long, lost brothers. (They also happen to live in a cave in Wales.) Imogen becomes too ill to accompany Belarius and his sons on a hunting trip. On their hunting trip, one of the sons, Guiderius, kills Imogen's oafish step-brother, Cloten, beheading him, after Cloten had provoked a fight "to the death" with Guiderius. While this is happening, Imogen succumbs "as if dead" in the cave, and when the men return, they find her, and they do believe she is dead. They leave the bodies of Imogen and Cloten together for burial. When Imogen regains consciousness, she is alone with the headless body of Cloten. Cloten is dressed in Posthumus' clothing. Therefore, Imogen assumes that this headless body is that of her beloved husband rather than the body of her detested and silly step-brother.

Imogen is a true heroine of a fairy-tale in which time touches little and improbabilities and incongruities touch all.

IMOGEN

[*Awakes.*] Yes, sir, to Milford-Haven, which is the way?
I thank you—By yond bush?—Pray how far thither?
'Ods pittikins! can it be six miles yet?—
I have gone all night. Faith, I'll lie down and sleep.
But soft! no bedfellow!—O gods and goddesses!
          [*Seeing the body of Cloten.*]
These flowers are like the pleasures of the world;
This bloody man, the care on't. I hope to dream;
For so I thought I was a cave-keeper,
And cook to honest creatures. But 'tis not so;

'Twas but a bolt of nothing, shot at nothing,
Which the brain makes of fumes: our very eyes
Are sometimes like our judgements, blind. Good faith,
I tremble still with fear: but if there be
Yet left in heaven as small a drop of pity
As a wren's eye, fear'd gods, a part of it!
The dream's here still: even when I wake it is
Without me, as within me; not imagin'd, felt.
A headless man! The garments of Posthumus!
I know the shape of's leg: this is his hand;
His foot Mercurical; his Martial thigh;
The brawns of Hercules: but his jovial face—
Murder in heaven? How—? 'Tis gone. Pisanio,
All curses madded Hecuba gave the Greeks,
And mine to boot, be darted on thee! Thou,
Conspir'd with that irregulous devil, Cloten,
Hast here cut off my lord. To write and read
Be henceforth treacherous! Damn'd Pisanio
Hath with his forged letters—damn'd Pisanio—
From this most bravest vessel of the world
Struck the main-top! O Posthumus! alas,
Where is thy head? where's that? Ay me! where's that?
Pisanio might have kill'd thee at the heart,
And left this head on. How should this be? Pisanio?
'Tis he and Cloten: malice and lucre in them
Have laid this woe here. O, 'tis pregnant, pregnant!
The drug he gave me, which he said was precious
And cordial to me, have I not found it
Murderous to the senses? That confirms it home:
This is Pisanio's deed, and Cloten's—O!
Give colour to my pale cheek with thy blood,
That we the horrider may seem to those
Which chance to find us. O, my lord! my lord!
                    [*Falls on the body.*]

A WINTER'S TALE
HERMIONE—ACT III, SCENE 2

AGE: Young   INTENT: Serious

The Winter's Tale is a play full of passion and the pain of jealously. It is full of grief and sensational surprises. It is full of romance and delights of the human comedy. It is also a pastoral. It is one of the two masterpieces Shakespeare wrote late in his career which deals with the theme of forgiveness.

In modern parlance, Leontes, King of Sicillia, is psychotic. He might possibly also be schizophrenic, but he is at least psychotically jealous of his wife, Hermione. He accuses her of adultery with his closest childhood friend, Polixenes, King of Bohemia. Leontes is convinced the child Hermione carries is not his, but a bastard fathered by Polixenes. When the baby girl is born, Leontes condemns the child to be transported, exposed, and abandoned on some deserted coast out of his realm. He also sends to the Oracle at Delos to ask Apollo to confirm his suspicions. Leontes brings Hermione to "trial," and she is cited for her "adultry" before a court of "justice."

Hermione proves herself a queen and the daughter of an "Emperor of Russia." She does not petition Leontes, nor does she bend to him. Her speech and carriage are dignified, as she constrains her sense of outrage. It is in these moments that she shows herself to be a woman of eminent nobility mingled with sweetness, a woman of greathearted strength and composure.

HERMIONE

Since what I am to say must be but that
Which contradicts my accusation and
The testimony of my part no other
But what comes from myself, it shall scarce boot me
To say 'not guilty': mine integrity
Being counted falsehood, shall, as I express it,
Be so received. But thus: if powers divine
Behold our human actions, as they do,
I doubt not then but innocence shall make

False accusation blush and tyranny
Tremble at patience. You, my lord, best know,
Who least will seem to do so, my past life
Hath been as continent, as chaste, as true,
As I am now unhappy; which is more
Than history can pattern, though devised
And play'd to take spectators. For behold me
A fellow of the royal bed, which owe
A moiety of the throne, a great king's daughter,
The mother to a hopeful prince, here standing
To prate and talk for life and honour 'fore
Who please to come and hear. For life, I prize it
As I weigh grief, which I would spare: for honour,
'Tis a derivative from me to mine,
And only that I stand for. I appeal
To your own conscience, sir, before Polixenes
Came to your court, how I was in your grace,
How merited to be so; since he came,
With what encounter so uncurrent I
Have strain'd to appear thus: if one jot beyond
The bound of honour, or in act or will
That way inclining, harden'd be the hearts
Of all that hear me, and my near'st of kin
Cry fie upon my grave!
          For Polixenes,
With whom I am accused, I do confess
I loved him as in honour he required,
With such a kind of love as might become
A lady like me, with a love even such,
So and no other, as yourself commanded:
Which not to have done I think had been in me
Both disobedience and ingratitude
To you and toward your friend, whose love had spoke,
Even since it could speak, from an infant, freely
That it was yours. Now, for conspiracy,
I know not how it tastes; though it be dish'd
For me to try how: all I know of it
Is that Camillo was an honest man;

And why he left your court, the gods themselves
Wotting no more than I, are ignorant.
                    Sir, spare your threats:
The bug which you would fright me with I seek.
To me can life be no commodity:
The crown and comfort of my life, your favour,
I do give lost; for I do feel it gone,
But know not how it went. My second joy
And first-fruits of my body, from his presence
I am barr'd, like one infectious. My third comfort,
Starr'd most unluckily, is from my breast,
The innocent milk in its most innocent mouth,
Haled out to murder: myself on every post
Proclaim'd a strumpet: with immodest hatred
The child-bed privilege denied, which 'longs
To women of all fashion; lastly, hurried
Here to this place, i' the open air, before
I have got strength of limit. Now, my liege,
Tell me what blessings I have here alive,
That I should fear to die? Therefore proceed.
But yet hear this; mistake me not; no life,
I prize it not a straw, but for mine honour,
Which I would free, if I shall be condemn'd
Upon surmises, all proofs sleeping else
But what your jealousies awake, I tell you
'Tis rigour and not law. Your honours all,
I do refer me to the oracle:
Apollo be my judge!

THE WINTER'S TALE
PAULINA—ACT III, SCENE 2

AGE: Mature [Any age]   INTENT: Serious

Toward the end of Hermione's "trial," the messengers whom Leontes had sent to Apollo's Oracle at Delos return with the god's message. Apollo, though his Oracle, declares that Hermione is "chaste," and that the babe is the King's, and that the King shall "live without heir if that which is lost be not found." Leontes refutes the Oracle, calling it all "falsehoods." Within moments of his pronouncement, the news is brought that the young son of the King and Hermione, Mamallus, is dead. Hermione is over-come. Within minutes, Paulina reports to Leontes that the Queen is dead from grief at this news.

Paulina is a lady of the court and wife to Lord Antigonus, one of the king's loyal lords. Paulina has been Hermione's staunchest defender at the court and against Leontes' accusations. Paulina is a termagant, but she is the most honorable, loyal, the bravest, and the wisest termagant one would care to know. Early on, she has understood that Leontes is ill, and she refers to his illness as his "lunes."

PAULINA

Woe the while!
O, cut my lace, lest my heart, cracking it,
Break too!
What studied torments, tyrant, hast for me?
What wheels? racks? fires? what flaying? boiling?
In leads or oils? what old or newer torture
Must I receive, whose every word deserves
To taste of thy most worst? Thy tyranny
Together working with thy jealousies,
Fancies too weak for boys, too green and idle
For girls of nine, O, think what they have done
And then run mad indeed, stark mad! for all
Thy by-gone fooleries were but spices of it.
That thou betray'dst Polixenes, 'twas nothing;

That but did show thee, of a fool, inconstant
And damnable ingrateful: nor was 't much,
Thou wouldst have poison'd good Camillo's honour,
To have him kill a king; poor trespasses,
More monstrous standing by: whereof I reckon
The casting forth to crows thy baby-daughter
To be or none or little; though a devil
Would have shed water out of fire ere done't:
Nor is't directly laid to thee, the death
Of the young prince, whose honourable thoughts,
Thoughts high for one so tender, cleft the heart
That could conceive a gross and foolish sire
Blemish'd his gracious dam: this is not, no,
Laid to thy answer: but the last,—O lords,
When I have said, cry 'woe!'—the queen , the queen,
The sweet'st, dear'st creature's dead and vengeance for't
Not dropped down yet.
I say she's dead: I'll swear't. If word nor oath
Prevail not, go and see: if you can bring
Tincture of lustre in her lip, her eye,
Heat outwardly or breath within, I'll serve you
As I would do the gods. But, O thou tyrant!
Do not repent these things, for they are heavier
Than all thy woes can stir: therefore betake thee
To nothing but despair. At thousand knees
Ten thousand years together, naked, fasting,
Upon a barren mountain, and still winter
In storm perpetual, could not move the gods
To look that way thou wert.
All faults I make, when I shall come to know them,
I do repent. Alas! I have show'd too much
The rashness of a woman: he is touch'd
To the noble heart. What's gone and what's past help
Should be past grief: do not receive affliction
At my petition; I beseech you, rather
Let me be punish'd, that have minded you
Of what you should forget. Now, good my liege,
Sir, royal sir, forgive a foolish woman:

The love I bore your queen —lo, fool again!—
I'll speak of her no more, nor of your children;
I'll not remember you of my own lord,
Who is lost too: take your patience to you,
And I'll say nothing.

THE WINTER'S TALE
ANTIGONUS—ACT III, SCENE 3

AGE: Mature [Any age]   INTENT: Serious

Antigonus is a lord attendant to Leontes, King of Sicillia. He is also the husband of Paulina. For whatever his own perverse reasons, Leontes orders Antigonus to take the newly born princess, born to Hermione and rejected by Leontes as his child, to "some remote and deserted place" and to "leave it without more mercy, to it's own protection and favour of the climate." Antigonus, as the king's liege-man, must obey. (Perhaps Leontes has chosen Antigonus for this distasteful mission because Paulina has confronted Leontes so harshly at every turn, and Leontes is therefore testing Antigonus' loyalty.) Antigonus brings the baby to a deserted and remote section of the sea-coast of Bohemia. He places the baby, unprotected on the beach.

ANTIGONUS

Come, poor babe:
I have heard, but not believed, the spirits o' the dead
May walk again: if such thing be, thy mother
Appear'd to me last night, for ne'er was dream
So like waking. To me comes a creature,
Sometimes her head on one side, some another;
I never saw a vessel of like sorrow,
So fill'd and so becoming: in pure white robes,
Like very sanctity, she did approach
My cabin where I lay; thrice bow'd before me,
And gasping to begin some speech, her eyes
Became two spouts: the fury spent, anon

Did this break from her: 'Good Antigonus,
Since fate, against thy better disposition
Hath made thy person the thrower-out
Of my poor babe, according to thine oath,
Places remote enough are in Bohemia,
There weep and leave it crying; and, for the babe
Is counted lost for ever, Perdita,
I prithee, call't. For this ungentle business,
Put on thee by my lord, thou ne'er shalt see
They wife Paulina more.' And so, with shrieks,
She melted into air. Affrighted much,
I did in time collect myself and thought
This was so and no slumber. Dreams are toys:
Yet for this once, yea, superstitiously,
I will be squared by this. I do believe
Hermione hath suffer'd death, and that
Apollo would, this being indeed the issue
Of King Polixenes, it should here be laid,
Either for life or death, upon the earth
Of its right father. Blossom, speed thee well!
There lie, and there thy character: there these;
Which may, if fortune please, both breed thee, pretty,
And still rest thine. The storm begins: poor wretch,
That for thy mother's fault art thus exposed
To loss and what may follow! Weep I cannot,
But my heart bleeds; and most accursed am I
To be by oath enjoin'd to this. Farewell!
The day frowns more and more: thou'rt like to have
A lullaby too rough: I never saw
The heavens so dim by day. A savage clamour!
Well may I get aboard! This is the chase:
I am gone for ever.

THE HISTORIES

KING RICHARD II
KING RICHARD—ACT III, SCENE 3

AGE: Young   INTENT: Serious

K ing Richard II is a dissolute monarch. King since a child, Richard *expects* obeisance to his absolutism. While in power, Richard is oppressive, overbearing, and imperious. He has an overweening confidence in his "divine right" as king, and a total belief that his subjects will respect this divine right. Richard allows his personal resentments, his own sense of injury, and his private motives to influence the justice he metes out as a sovereign. Richard's greatest failure as a monarch, however, is that he *can not be trusted*. He makes a fundamental mistake by withholding, for personal reasons, Henry Bolingbroke's inheritance as the new Duke of Lancaster. This causes an already alienated nobility to be even more insecure towards Richard as their King. Richard *has* to go; and in Bolingbroke the other nobles find a leader able to overthrow this irresponsible ruler.

Richard has returned from his disastrous wars in Ireland to find a kingdom filled with strife and insurgency. And Bolingbroke has easily gained the upper hand. He has already executed Richard's closest friends, and the rebel nobles have cornered the King and his meager force at Flint Castle in Wales. Bolingbroke has sent the Earl of Northumberland to negotiate the King's surrender. From the castle's battlements, in a moment too late in his reign to be effective, Richard summons the stature to be right regal and to appear to be a king who is capable of commanding and ruling as well as reigning. Richard verbally defies his opponents and for once sounds like the sovereign that he always should have been.

KING RICHARD

We are amazed; and thus long we have stood
To watch the fearful bending of thy knee,
Because we thought ourself thy lawful king:
And if we be, how dare thy joints forget

To pay their awful duty to our presence?
If we be not, show us the hand of God
That hath dismiss'd us from our stewardship;
For well we know, no hand of blood and bone
Can gripe the sacred handle of our sceptre,
Unless he do profane, steal, or usurp.
And though you think that all, as you have done,
Have torn their souls by turning them from us,
And we are barren and bereft of friends;
Yet know, my master, God omnipotent,
Is mustering in his clouds in our behalf
Armies of pestilence; and they shall strike
Your children yet unborn and unbegot,
That lift your vassal hands against my head
And threat the glory of my precious crown.
Tell Bolingbroke—for yond methinks he stands—
That every stride he makes upon my land
Is dangerous treason: he is come to open
The purple testament of bleeding war;
But ere the crown he looks for live in peace,
Ten thousand bloody crowns of mothers' sons
Shall ill become the flower of England's face,
Change the complexion of her maid-pale peace
To scarlet indignation and bedew
Her pastures' grass with faithful English blood.

KING HENRY IV, PART II
MISTRESS QUICKLY—ACT II, SCENE 1

AGE: Mature [Any age]   INTENT: Humorous

King Henyry IV, Part II is probably one of the finest blendings of
comedy and human drama that Shakespeare achieved. The play is
dominated by Sir John Falstaff, to the point that some wags have
stated that the play would be better titled "*Falstaff.*" The scenes which
occupy the low-life that surrounds Falstaff, Justice Shallow, Mistress
Quickly, and the "patrons" of the Boar's Head Tavern are "social real-

ism" of the Elizabethan time beyond compare. They contain disgrace and bawdiness, vividness and vitality; they have, too, their poetry and pathos. These scenes are full of intense humanity. And in the play they occupy greater stage-time than the rebellion of Northumberland and Archbishop Scroop and the father/son relationship of King Henry and Prince Hal combined, which appears to be the main business of the chronicle's plot.

Mistress Quickly is the "hostess" of the Boar's Head Tavern in Eastcheap where Falstaff makes his headquarters. She is an earthy woman and by circumstances a fishwife, but when one considers her days and nights are spent in constant companionship with Falstaff and his crew of thieves and rogues, it is not hard to understand why she is. Mistress Quickly has brought suit and action against Falstaff for money owed her and for his broken promise of marriage to her. She has brought with her Fang and Snare, two of the sheriff's men, to arrest Falstaff and bring him to court. Falstaff and his motley crew resist and draw swords. Into this fracas comes the Lord Chief Justice of the King's bench.

MISTRESS QUICKLY

[To Falstaff.]
Throw me in the channel! I'll throw thee in the channel. Wilt thou? wilt thou? thou bastardly rogue! Murder, murder! ah, thou honey-suckled villain! wilt thou kill God's officers and the king's? Ah, thou honey-seed rogue! thou art a honey-seed! a man-queller, and a woman-queller.
Good people, bring a rescue or two. Thou wo't, wo't thou? thou wo't wo't ta? do, do, thou rogue! do, thou hemp-seed!
[Enter the Lord Chief Justice, and his men.]
Good my lord, be good to me. I beseech you, stand to me.
O my most worshipful lord, an't please your grace, I am a poor widow of Eastcheap, and he is a arrested at my suit.
It is more than for some, my lord; it is for all, all I have. He hath eaten me out of house and home; he hath put all my substance into that fat belly of his: but I will have some of it out again, or I will ride thee o' nights like the mare.
[To Falstaff.]

Marry, if thou wert an honest man, thyself and the money too. Thou didst swear to me upon a parcel-gilt goblet, sitting in my Dolphin-chamber, at the round table, by the sea-coal fire, upon Wednesday in Wheeson week, when the prince broke thy head for liking his father to a singingman of Windsor, thou didst swear to me then, as I was washing thy wound, to marry me and make me my lady thy wife. Canst thou deny it? Did not goodwife Keech, the butcher's wife, come in then and call me gossip Quickly? coming in to borrow a mess of vinegar: telling us she had a good dish of prawns; wherby thou didst desire to eat some; whereby I told thee they were ill for a green wound? And didst thou not, when she was gone down stairs, desire me to be no more so familiarity with such poor people; saying that ere long they should call me madam? And didst thou not kiss me and bid me fetch thee thirty shillings? I put thee now to thy book-oath: deny it, if thou canst.

KING HENRY IV, PART II
LADY PERCY—ACT II, SCENE 3

AGE: Young [Any age]   INTENT: Serious

L ady Percy is the widow of Harry Percy ("Hotspur"), whom Prince Hal killed in single combat at the Battle of Shrewsbury (*King Henry IV, Part I*). She is the daughter-in-law of the Earl of Northumberland, who joined forces with King Henry when he rebelled against Richard II; and, then, when the Percys felt slighted, lead a rebellion against Henry (*King Henry IV, Part I*). Northumberland played "crafty-sick" at the Battle of Shrewsbury and failed to bring up his power to aid his son and their allies, which contributed to the King's victory over them. Now, Northumberland prepares to join forces with the Archbishop of York in still another insurrection against the Crown. Lady Northumberland is resigned to her husband's decision, but Lady Percy is not so much concerned with the safety of Northumberland as she is that he will do for others what he would not do for his own son: support in battle. Northumberland had been responsible for making her a widow and leaving her bereft of her adored husband.

LADY PERCY

O yet, for God's sake, go not to these wars!
The time was, father, that you broke your word,
When you were more endear'd to it than now;
When your own Percy, when my heart's dear Harry,
Threw many a northward look to see his father
Bring up his powers; but he did long in vain.
Who then persuaded you to stay at home?
There were two honors lost, yours and your son's.
For yours, the God of heaven brighten it!
For his, it stuck upon him as the sun
In the grey vault of heaven, and by his light
Did all chivalry of England move
To do brave acts: he was indeed the glass
Wherein the noble youth did dress themselves:
He had no legs that practised not his gait;
And speaking thick, which nature made his blemish,
Became the accents of the valiant;
For those that could speak low and tardily
Would turn their own perfection to abuse,
To seem like him: so that in speech, in gait,
In diet, in affections of delight,
In military rules, humours of blood,
He was the mark and glass, copy and book,
That fashion'd others. And him, O wondrous him!
O miracle of men! him did you leave,
Second to none, unseconded by you,
To look upon the hideous god of war
In disadvantage; to abide a field
Where nothing but the sound of Hotspur's name
Did seem defensible: so you left him.
Never, O never, do his ghost the wrong
To hold your honour more precise and nice
With others than with him! Let them alone:
The marshall and the archbishop are strong:
Had my sweet Harry had but half their numbers,
To-day might I, hanging on Hotspur's neck,

Have talk'd of Monmouth's grave.
If they get ground and vantage of the king,
Then join you with them, like a rib of steel,
To make strength stronger; but, for all our loves,
First let them try themselves. So did your son;
He was so suffer'd: so came I a widow;
And never shall have length of life enough
To rain upon remembrance with mine eyes,
That it may grow and sprout as high as heaven,
For recordation to my noble husband.

KING HENRY IV, PART II
KING HENRY—ACT III, SCENE 1

AGE: Mature   INTENT: Serious

King Henry IV is a care-worn man, a troubled monarch, and a
worried and anxious father. He is also ill and aging. King Henry
suffers from insomnia and longs for sleep to give him a brief peace
from his world for a while. He is a man of his time—a Medieval man.
He is inflicted with a terrible sense of guilt over the way he gained the
throne and the subsequent murder of his cousin, King Richard II.
Henry longs to expiate his guilt by going on a Holy Crusade. He
believes that both his troubled kingdom and his troubled family are
forms of retribution inflicted upon him from his previous acts. For
most of his reign, England has been in turmoil and civil strife. Yet
King Henry has done all he has to give his heir, Prince Hal, a firmer
hold on the throne when he comes to it. And no matter how often Hal
proves himself in battle, King Henry still has nagging doubts about his
son's fitness to be king because of his continued association with
Falstaff and his fear that Hal may not have the attributes to make a
worthy king (Prince Hal was more fond of King Richard II as a boy
then he was of his own father). He also wonders if Hal wishes to seize
the crown from his father before his father is dead (Hal would not be
the first prince to wish to supplant his father on a throne). Yet, for all
of his personal wishes, King Henry accepts his title and his
circumstances. He is King of England and head of a government.

KING HENRY

How many thousand of my poorest subjects
Are at this hour asleep! O sleep, O gentle sleep,
Nature's soft nurse, how have I frightened thee,
That thou no more wilt weigh my eyelids down
And steep my senses in forgetfulness?
Why rather, sleep, liest thou in smoky cribs,
Upon uneasy pallets stretching thee
And hush'd with buzzing night-flies to thy slumber,
Than in the perfumed chambers of the great,
Under the canopies of costly state,
And lull'd with sound of sweetest melody?
O thou dull god, why liest thou with the vile
In loathsome beds, and leavest the kingly couch
A watch-case or a common 'larum-bell?
Wilt thou upon the high and giddy mast
Seal up the ship-boy's eyes, and rock his brains
In cradle of the rude imperious surge
And in the visitations of the winds,
Who take the ruffian billows by the top,
Curling their monstrous heads and hanging them
With deafening clamour in the slippery clouds,
That, with the hurly, death itself awakes?
Canst thou, O partial sleep, give thy repose
To the wet sea-boy in an hour so rude,
And in the calmest and most stillest night,
With all appliances and means to boot,
Deny it to a king? Then happy low, lie down!
Uneasy lies the had that wears a crown.

KING HENRY IV, PART II
FALSTAFF—ACT IV, SCENE 3

AGE: Mature   INTENT: Humorous

Falstaff is a coward; he is a braggart; but he is no fool. He is wise enough to know why Prince Hal has kept him as a companion: it is Falstaff's function to keep the Prince in laughter.

With his usual impeccable timing for missing a battle and arriving just at the end of it, Falstaff appears at Gaultree Forest, Yorkshire, just as the rebel forces are defeated by the royal army under the command of Prince John of Lancaster, King Henry's second son. Prince John is a sober young man, much like his father, and he has no patience with Falstaff, nor with his bragging and roguish ways. When Falstaff learns Prince John is to return immediately to court, because the king is "sick," Falstaff tries to ingratiate himself to Prince John by asking that the prince, when he comes to court, to "Stand my good lord, pray, in your good report." Prince John leaves Falstaff with the parting remark that he will speak better of Falstaff than Falstaff deserves.

FALSTAFF

I would you had but the wit: 'twere better than your dukedom. Good faith, this same young sober-blooded boy doth not love me; nor a man cannot make him laugh; but that's no marvel, he drinks no wine. There's never none of these demure boys come to any proof; for thin drink doth so over-cool their blood, and making many fish-meals, that they fall into a kind of male green-sickness; and then, when they marry, they get wenches: they are generally fools and cowards; which some of us should be too, but for inflammation. A good sherris-sack hath a two-fold operation in it. It ascends me into the brain: dries me there all the foolish and full and crudy vapours which environ it; makes it apprehensive, quick, forgetive, full of nimble fiery and delectable shapes; which, delivered o'er to the voice, the tongue, which is the birth, becomes excellent wit. The second property of your excellent sherris is, the warming of the blood; which, before cold and settled, left the liver white and pale, which is the badge of pusillanimity and cowardice; but the sherris warms it and makes it course from the inwards to parts extreme: it illumineth the face, which as a beacon gives warning to all the rest of this little kingdom, man, to arm; and then the vital commoners and inland petty spirits muster me all to their captain, the heart, who, great and puffed up with this retinue, doth any deed of courage; and this valour comes of sherris. So that skill in the weapon is nothing without sack, for that sets it a-work; and learning a mere hoard of gold kept by a devil, till sack commences it and sets it in act and use. Hereof comes it that Prince Harry is valiant; for the cold blood he did naturally inherit of his father, he hath, like lean, sterile and bare land, manured, husbanded and tilled with excellent endeavour of drinking good and good store of fertile sherris, that he is become very hot and valiant. If I had a thousand sons the first humane principle I would teach them should be, to forswear thin potations and to addict themselves to sack.

KING HENRY V
KING HENRY—ACT V, SCENE 2

AGE: Young   INTENT: Humorous

King Henry V, both as prince and king, was a hero to the Elizabethans. They were fascinated by his complex and compelling character. In tracing the growth of this character in both *King Henry IV, Paarts I & II*, and *King Henry V*, it is not hard to believe that Henry V was the one character from English history whom Shakespeare loved and admired above all others. His Henry grows from raucous prince to Ideal King. Shakespeare's Henry V is a warrior of skill, leadership, and bravery, able to inspire his men to go beyond their capacity. He is the justice-minded sovereign who places the good of his people and kingdom above his own needs. He is the general who questions his responsibility for the deaths of his fighting men. Shakespeare makes for his audience a hero.

But Shakespeare ends his chronicle by giving his audience still another Henry. As Henry woos Katherine of France, Shakespeare presents a very vulnerable Henry. He shows Henry the Man, who is amusing and charming as he finds himself in the most emotionally exposed of circumstances: a man trying to create a relationship with a

woman. This is Shakespeare's Human Henry. This final Henry is one
with whom the groundlings can empathize as well as admire. And to
make sure there is no mistake that this is Henry the Common Man and
not Henry the Ideal King, Shakespeare writes the scene in prose, not in
lofty, poetic verse.

KING HENRY

O fair Katherine, if you will love me soundly with your French heart, I
will be glad to hear you confess it brokenly in your English tongue.
Do you like me, Kate? I' faith, Kate, my wooing is fit for thy
understanding: I am glad thou canst speak no better English; for, if
thou couldst, thou wouldst find me such a plain king that thou wouldst
think I had sold my farm to buy my crown. I know no ways to mince it
in love, but directly to say 'I love you': then if you urge me farther
than to say 'do you in faith?' I wear out my suit. Give me your
answer; i' faith, do: and so clap hands and a bargain: how say you,
lady? Marry, if you would put me to verses or to dance for your sake,
Kate, why you undid me: for the one, I have neither words nor
measure, and for the other, I have no strength in measure, yet a
reasonable measure in strength. If I could win a lady at leap-frog, or
by vaulting into my saddle with my armour on my back, under the
correction of bragging be it spoken, I should quickly leap into a wife.
Or if I might buffet for my love, or bound my horse for her favours, I
could lay on like a butcher and sit like a jack-an-apes, never off. But,
before God, Kate, I cannot look greenly nor gasp out my eloquence,
nor I have no cunning in protestation; only downright oaths, which I
never use till urged nor never break for urging. If thou canst love a
fellow of this temper, Kate, whose face is not worth sunburning, that
never looks in his glass for love of any thing he sees there, let thine
eye be thy cook. I speak to thee plain soldier: if thou canst love me for
this, take me; if not, to say to thee that I shall die, is true; but for thy
love, by the Lord, no; yet I love thee too. And while thou livest, dear
Kate, take a fellow of plain and uncoined constancy; for he perforce
must do thee right, because he hath not the gift to woo in other places;
for these fellows of infinite tongue, that can rhyme themselves into
ladies' favours, they do always reason themselves out again. What! a
speaker is but a prater; a rhyme is but a ballad. A good leg will fall; a

straight back will stoop; a black beard will turn white; a curled pate will grow bald; a fair face will wither; a full eye will wax hollow: but a good heart, Kate, is the sun and the moon; or rather the sun and not the moon; for it shines bright and never changes, but keeps his course truly. If thou would have such a one, take me; and take me, take a soldier; take a soldier, take a king. And what sayest thou then to my love? speak, my fair, and fairly, I pray thee.

KING HENRY VI, PART II
DUCHESS OF GLOUCESTER—ACT II, SCENE 4

AGE: Mature [Any age]   INTENT: Serious

Humphrey, Duke of Gloucester, was the younger brother of King Henry V, and Lord Protector of England and King Henry VI during his long minority reign. Gloucester was popular with the people, but, in the KING HENRY VI plays, not with Margaret of Anjou and her faction, once she came to court. The Duchess of Gloucester was known for her beauty—and her ambition. She wanted to be Queen of England, and in the plays she resorts to witchcraft and the conjuring of spirits in order to gain this ambition. She is caught, tried, but, because of her rank, is banished for life rather than be burned at the stake.

Before she is exiled to the Isle of Man, however, the Duchess must do "three days of open penance." This means she must wander for three days through the cities and countryside, barefoot, clad only in a white sheet, exposed to the abuse and chiding of both the elements and the people. On the last day of her penance, before she leaves for exile, the Duchess, bruised but not beaten, meets her husband for the last time. They are on a street.

DUCHESS OF GLOUCESTER

Come you, my lord, to see my open shame?
Now thou does penance too. Look how they gaze!
See how the giddy multitude do point,
And nod their heads, and throw their eyes on thee!

Ah, Gloucester, hide thee from their hateful looks,
And, in thy closet pent up, rue my shame,
And ban thine enemies, both mine and thine!
Ah, Gloucester, teach me to forget myself!
For whilst I think I am thy married wife
And thou a prince, protector of this land,
Methinks I should not thus be led along,
Mail'd up in shame, with papers on my back,
And follow'd with a rabble that rejoice
To see my tears and hear my deep-fet groans.
The ruthless flint doth cut my tender feet,
And when I start, the envious people laugh
And bid me be advised how I tread.
Ah, Humphrey, can I bear this shameful yoke?
Trow'st thou that e'er I'll look upon the world,
Or count them happy that enjoy the sun?
No; dark shall be my light and night my day;
To think upon my pomp shall be my hell.
Sometime I'll say, I am Duke Humphrey's wife,
And he a prince and ruler of the land:
Yet so he ruled and such a prince he was
As he stood by whilst I, his forlorn duchess,
Was made a wonder and a pointing-stock
To every idle rascal follower.
But be thou mild and blush not at my shame,
Nor stir at nothing till the axe of death
Hang over thee, as, sure, it shortly will;
For Suffolk, he that can do all in all
With her that hateth thee and hates us all,
And York and impious Beaufort, that false priest,
Have all limed bushes to betray thy wings,
And, fly thou how thou canst, they'll tangle thee:
But fear not thou, until thy foot is snared.
Nor never seek prevention of thy foes.
        [*Exeunt Gloucester and his Serving men.*]
Art thou gone too? all comfort go with thee!
For none abides with me: my joy is death;
Death, at whose name I oft have been afear'd,

Because I wish'd this world's eternity.
Stanley, I prithee, go, and take me hence;
I care not whither, for I beg no favour,
Only convey me where thou are commanded.
My shame will not be shifted with my sheet;
No, it will hang upon my richest robes
And show itself, attire me how I can.
Go, lead the way; I long to see my prison.

KING HENRY VI, PART II
YOUNG CLIFFORD—ACT V, SCENE 2

AGE: Young   INTENT: Serious

The Cliffords were partisans of Henry VI. Historically, Young
Clifford was the great-grandson of Harry Percy ("Hotspur"), and
from Shakespeare's depiction of him in this play, he was just as
impetuous and hot-headed in battle as his famous ancestor.

The place is the battle field of St. Albans, a decisive encounter in
the War of the Roses in which the Yorkists defeated the Lancastrian
forces under Queen Margaret. Young Clifford's father is killed by the
Duke of York in a battlefield duel. Young Clifford, inspired by battle
and shamed by the Lancastrian loss and retreat, remains on the field
still searching for glory and victory at any cost, much like his famous
great-grandsire did at the Battle of Shrewsbury. What Young Clifford
finds is the still warm body of his father, and his blood hot for victory
turns to blood cold for revenge.

YOUNG CLIFFORD

Shame and confusion! all is on the rout;
Fear frames disorder, and disorder wounds
Where it should guard. O war, thou son of hell,
Whom angry heavens do make their minister,
Throw in the frozen bosoms of our part
Hot coals of vengeance! Let no soldier fly.
He that is truly dedicate to war

Hath no self-love, nor he that loves himself
Hath not essentially but by circumstance
The name of valour. [*Seeing his dead father.*]
    O, let the vile world end,
And the premised flames of the last day
Knit earth and heaven together!
Now let the general trumpet blow his blast,
Particularities and petty sounds
To cease! Wast thou ordain'd, dear father,
To lose thy youth in peace, and to achieve
The silver livery of advised age,
And, in thy reverence and thy chair-days, thus
To die in ruffian battle? Even at this sight
My heart is turn'd to stone: and while 'tis mine,
It shall be stony. York not our old men spares;
No more will I their babes; tears virginal
Shall be to me even as the dew to fire;
And beauty that the tyrant oft reclaims,
Shall to my flaming wrath be oil and flax.
Henceforth I will not have to do with pity:
Meet I an infant of the house of York,
Into as many gobbets will I cut it
As wild Medea young Absyrtus did:
In cruelty will I seek out my fame.
Come, thou new ruin of old Clifford's house:
As did Aeneas old Anchises bear,
So bear I thee upon my manly shoulders;
But then Aeneas bare a living load,
Nothing so heavy as these woes of mine.

KING HENRY VI, PART III
QUEEN MARGARET—ACT I, SCENE 4

AGE: Mature   INTENT: Serious

Queen Margaret is the dominate female figure in the Henry VI plays. She is unprincipled, revengeful, coarse, fierce, audacious, and a virago. She is contemptuous of her husband, the gentle and imbecilic King Henry VI, and she resents (and rightly so) her husband when he disinherits their son in favor of Richard, Duke of York, and his heirs to inherit the English crown. Her wrath causes her to raise an army, and she defeats the Yorkists at the Battle of Wakefield. In this battle her forces capture the Duke of York.

York has been brought before Queen Margaret, guarded by the Earl of Northumberland and Lord Clifford (the young Clifford of the Battle of St. Albans in *King Henry VI, Part II*). This is the moment of Margaret's greatest triumph so far—and the moment she has long anticipated for her revenge.

QUEEN MARGARET

Hold, valiant Clifford! for a thousand causes
I would prolong awhile the traitor's life.
Brave warriors, Clifford and Northumberland,
Come, make him stand upon this molehill here,
That raught at mountains with outstretched arms,
Yet parted but the shadow with his hand.
What! was it you that would be England's king?
Was't you that revell'd in our parliament,
And made a preachment of our high descent?
Where are your mess of sons to back you now?
The wanton Edward, and the lusty George?
And where's that valiant crook-back prodigy,
Dicky your boy, that with his grumbling voice
Was wont to cheer his dad in mutinies?
Or, with the rest, where is your darling Rutland?
Look, York: I stain'd this napkin with the blood
That valiant Clifford, with his rapier's point,

Made issue from the bosom of the boy;
And if thine eyes can water for his death,
I give you this to dry thy cheeks withal.
Alas, poor York! but that I hate thee deadly,
I should lament thy miserable state.
I prithee, grieve, to make me merry, York.
What, hath thy fiery heart so parch'd thine entrails
That not a tear can fall for Rutland's death?
Why art thou patient, man? Thou shouldst be mad;
And I, to make thee mad, do mock thee thus.
Stamp, rave, and fret, that I may sing and dance.
Thou wouldst be fee'd, I see, to make me sport:
York cannot speak, unless he wear a crown.
A crown for York! and, lords, bow low to him:
Hold you his hands, whilst I do set it on.
          [*Putting a paper crown on his head.*]
Ay, marry, sir, now looks he like a king!
Ay, this is he that took King Henry's chair,
And this is he was his adopted heir.
But how is it that great Plantagenet
Is crown'd so soon, and broke his solemn oath?
As I bethink me, you should not be king
Till our Henry had shook hands with death.
And will you pale your head in Henry's glory,
And rob his temples of the diadem,
Now in his life, against your holy oath?
O, 'tis a fault too too unpardonable!
Off with the crown; and, with the crown, his head;
And, whilst we breathe, take time to do him dead.

KING HENRY VIII
QUEEN KATHARINE — ACT II, SCENE 4

AGE: Mature   INTENT: Serious

Katharine of Aragon, first wife of King Henry VIII, is a noble and dignified woman, and she is always a queen. She was a princess of Spain, daughter of Ferdinand and Isabella, and for nearly a quarter of a century Queen of England. Her pride of birth and her sense of her station never desert her. In the play, these qualities of character are mingled and united with a capacity for long-enduring affection and with a religious meekness. All together they blend to give a noble dignity and a gentle pathos to her words and to her struggle to maintain the position and the rank to which she feels she has a right.

Katharine has been called, as Queen of England, to a hall in Blackfriars, to a kangaroo ecclesiastical court to be divorced on religious grounds from King Henry VIII. Rather than answer the ceremonial cry of "Say, Katharine Queen of England, come into the court," with the customary "Here," Katharine makes no answer. Instead, silently, she rises from her place, makes a progress about the court, and ends at the feet of Henry, sitting under a cloth of state, where she kneels as a petitioner.

QUEEN KATHARINE

Sir, I desire you do me right and justice;
And to bestow your pity on me: for
I am a most poor woman, and a stranger,
Born out of your dominions; having here
No judge indifferent, nor no more assurance
Of equal friendship and proceeding. Alas, sir,
In what have I offended you? what cause
Hath my behaviour given your displeasure,
That thus you should to proceed to put me off,
And take your good grace from me? Heaven witness,
I have been to you a true and humble wife,
At all times to your will conformable:
Ever in fear to kindle your dislike,

Yea, subject to your countenance, glad or sorry
As I saw it inclined: when was the hour
I ever contradicted your desire,
Or made it not mine too? Or which of your friends
Have I not strove to love, although I knew
He were mine enemy? what friend of mine
That had to him derived your anger, did I
Continue in my liking? nay, gave notice
He was from thence discharged? Sir, call to mind
That I have been your wife, in this obedience,
Upward of twenty years, and have been blest
With many children by you: if, in the course
And process of this time, you can report,
And prove it too, against mine honour aught,
My bond to wedlock, or my love and duty,
Against your sacred person, in God's name,
Turn me away, and let the foul'st contempt
Shut door on me, and so give me up
To the sharp'st kind of justice. Please you, sir,
The king, your father, was reputed for
A prince most prudent, of an excellent
And unmatch'd wit and judgement: Ferdinand,
My father, king of Spain, was reckon'd one
The wisest prince that there had reign'd by many
A year before: it is not to be question'd
That they had gather'd a wise council to them
Of every realm, that did debate this business,
Who deem'd our marriage lawful: wherefore I humbly
Beseech you, sir, to spare me, till I may
Be by my friends in Spain advised; whose counsel
I will implore: if not, i' the name of God,
Your pleasure be fullfill'd!

THE TRAGEDIES

ROMEO and JULIET
FRIAR LAURENCE—ACT III, SCENE 3

AGE: Mature   INTENT: Serious

Friar Laurence, when he married Romeo Montague to Juliet Capulet, hoped their marriage—when made public—would end the blood-splattered feud of the two families. Unfortunately, within hours after Romeo married Juliet, he killed Tybalt, her cousin (and now his kinsman). Tybalt had just dispatched Romeo's friend, Mercutio; and in an irrational outburst, caused by uncontrolled, adolescent fury-cum-guilt, Romeo slew Tybalt in a street fight. His singular focus was to avenge Mercutio's death. In one, swift rapier's thrust, Romeo managed to break the Prince's edict against street brawling between the Montagues and Capulets; to get himself exiled from Verona on pain of death if he was found within the city by the next morning; to deepen the feud between the two families; and possibly to lose his love, his Juliet.

Romeo takes refuge in Friar Laurence's cell. When the good friar delivers the Prince's sentence of banishment, Romeo again reacts as a scared, panicked, and irrational teenager, not stopping to listen to the counsel of the friar. Finally, when Romeo in his desperation threatens rash suicide, Friar Laurence loses patience with the boy and badgers him to act the man his "form cries out" he is.

FRIAR LAURENCE

Hold thy desperate hand:
Art thou a man? thy form cries out thou art:
Thy tears are womanish; thy wild acts denote
The unreasonable fury of a beast:
Unseemly woman in a seeming man!
Or ill-beseeming beast in seeming both!
Thou has amazed me: by my holy order,
I thought thy disposition better temper'd.
Hast thou slain Tybalt? wilt thou slay thyself?

And slay thy lady too that lives in thee,
By doing damned hate upon thyself?
Why rail'st thou on thy birth, the heaven, and earth?
Since birth, and heaven, and earth, all three do meet
In thee at once; which thou at once wouldst lose.
Fie, fie, thou shamest thy shape, thy love, thy wit:
Which, like a usurer, abound'st in all,
And usest none in that true use indeed
Which should bedeck thy shape, thy love, thy wit:
Thy nobel shape is but a form of wax,
Digressing from the valour of a man;
Thy dear love sworn but hollow perjury,
Killing that love which thou hast vow'd to cherish;
Thy wit, that ornament to shape and love,
Mis-shapen in the conduct of them both,
Like powder in a skilless soldier's flask,
Is set a-fire by thine own ignorance,
And thou dismember'd with thine own defence.
What, rouse thee, man! thy Juliet is alive,
For whose dear sake thou wast but lately dead;
There art thou happy; Tybalt would kill thee,
But thou slew'st Tybalt; there art thou happy too:
The law that threaten'd death becomes thy friend
And turns it to exile; there are thou happy:
A pack of blessings lights upon thy back;
Happiness courts thee in her best array;
But, like a misbehaved and sullen wench,
Thou pout'st upon thy fortune and thy love:
Take heed, take heed, for such die miserable.
Go, get thee to thy love, as was decreed,
Ascend her chamber, hence and comfort her:
But look thou stay not till the watch be set,
For then thou canst not pass to Mantua:
Where thou shalt live, till we can find a time
To blaze your marriage, reconcile your friends,
Beg pardon of the prince, and call thee back
With twenty hundred thousand times more joy
Than thou went'st forth in lamentation.

Go before, nurse: commend me to thy lady;
And bid her hasten all the house to bed,
Which heavy sorrow makes them apt unto:
Romeo is coming.
Go hence; good night; and here stands all your state:
Either be gone before the watch is set,
Or by break of day disguised from hence:
Sojourn in Mantua; I'll find out your man,
And he shall signify from time to time
Every good hap to you that chances here:
Give me thy hand; 'tis late: farewell; good night.

ROMEO and JULIET
JULIET—ACT IV, SCENE 3

AGE: Young   INTENT: Serious

Juliet is approximately fourteen years old. She is the secret bride (and now consummated wife) of the exiled Romeo Montague. Of her household only her nurse knows that she is married. Therefore, Juliet's father has arranged that Juliet marry the Count Paris, a kinsman of the Prince of Verona. Juliet refuses to marry at first, but Lord Capulet orders his daughter to marry Count Paris or be shunned from his house forever. Juliet is distraught. She has been left emotionally alone, dangling over her garden from her balcony window: her young husband in exile in Mantua; her Nurse, who up to this point has supported her marriage to Romeo, has advised her to forget that marriage ever existed and to marry and to accept Paris as her only husband (a sin in the eyes of Heaven); and her mother and father simply expect her to accept their plans for her without question, like a good, obedient, dutiful daughter. In her desperation, Juliet turns to the only man she can: Friar Laurence. The friar is not only the one who performed the marriage rite and is her confessor, he is also an herbalist. He gives her a potion which will make her sleep for "two and forty hours," as if in death. At the end of that time, she shall wake, and he will see that she is rejoined with her Romeo. Despondent because of her situation, Juliet agrees to the plan.

Juilet is in her bedchamber. She has just bade goodnight to her
mother and nurse. She then contemplates the potion given her by the
Friar. After all that has happened to her, fears and doubts fill her soul.

JULIET

Farewell! God knows when we shall meet again.
I have a faint cold fear thrills through my veins,
That almost freezes up the heat of life:
I'll call them back again to comfort me:
Nurse! What should she do here?
My dismal scene I needs must act alone.
Come, vial.
What if this mixture do not work at all?
Shall I be married then to-morrow morning?
No, no: this shall forbid it: lie thou there.
                [*Laying down her dagger.*]
What if it be poison, which the friar
Subtly hath minister'd to have me dead,
Lest in this marriage he should be dishonour'd,
Because he married me before to Romeo?
I fear it is: and yet, methinks, it should not,
For he hath still been tried a holy man.
How if, when I am laid into the tomb,
I wake before the time that Romeo
Come to redeem me? there's a fearful point!
Shall I not, then, be stifled in the vault,
To whose foul mouth no healthsome air breathes in,
And there die strangled ere my Romeo comes?
Or, if I live, is it not very like,
The horrible conceit of death and night,
Together with the terror of the place,—
As in a vault, an ancient receptacle,
Where, for these many hundred years, the bones
Of all my buried ancestors are pack'd:
Where bloody Tybalt, yet but green in earth,
Lies festering in his shroud; where, as they say,
At some hours in the night spirits resort;—

Alack, alack, is it not like that I,
So early waking, what with loathsome smells,
And shrieks like mandrakes' torn out of the earth,
That living mortals, hearing them, run mad:—
O, if I wake, shall I not be distraught,
Environed with all these hideous fears?
And madly play with my forefathers' joints?
And pluck the mangled Tybalt from his shroud?
And, in this rage, with some great kinsman's bone,
As with a club, dash out my desperate brains?
O, look! methinks I see my cousin's ghost
Seeking out Romeo, that did spit his body
Upon a rapier's point: stay, Tybalt, stay!
Romeo, I come! this do I drink to thee.

ROMEO and JULIET
ROMEO—ACT V, SCENE 3

AGE: Young   INTENT: Serious

Romeo's manservant, Balthasar, has brought to his master in Mantua the news that all Verona knows: young Juliet Capulet is dead. What Romeo has not heard, because even Balthasar does not know, is the truth: that Juliet is alive, but just in an induced sleep which feigns death. Romeo acts once again like the impulsive, brash seventeen-year-old he is. Life without Juliet is not worth the effort. Without further thought, Romeo "defies the stars," and returns to Verona. He sneaks into the city's tombs during the dark of night, and there, in the Capulet's tombs, near the body of his wife, he intends to kill himself by taking poison which he procured from an apothecary in Mantua.

However, upon reaching the tombs he encounters another young man mourning Juliet and keeping watch at her tomb. The two duel, and Romeo once again vanquishes an opponent. After he has killed his adversary, Romeo recognizes him: Count Paris, Lord Capulet's choice for his daughter. Romeo then espies the body of Juliet. He bids his farewells, asks the dead for their forgiveness for his wrongs against them, and prepares to take his own life.

ROMEO

Let me peruse this face.
Mercutio's kinsman, noble County Paris!
What said my man, when my betossed soul
Did not attend him as we rode? I think
He told me Paris should have married Juliet:
Said he not so? or did I dream it so?
Or am I mad, hearing him talk of Juliet,
To think it was so? O, give me thy hand,
One writ with me in sour misfortune's book!
I'll bury thee in a triumphant grave;
A grave? O, no! a lantern, slaughter'd youth,
For here lies Juliet, and her beauty makes
This vault a feasting presence full of light.
Death, lie thou there, by a dead man interr'd.
                    [*Laying Paris in the tomb.*,]
How oft when men are at the point of death
Have they been merry! which their keepers call
A lightning before death: O, how may I
Call this lightning? O my love! my wife!
Death, that hath suck'd the honey of thy breath,
Hath no power yet upon thy beauty:
Thou art not conquer'd; beauty's ensign yet
Is crimson in thy lips and in thy cheeks,
And death's pale flag is not advanced there.
Tybalt, liest thou there in thy bloody sheet?
O, what more favour can I do to thee,
Than with that hand that cut thy youth in twain
To sunder his that was thine enemy?
Forgive me, cousin! Ah, dear Juliet,
Why art thou yet so fair? shall I believe
That unsubstantial death is amorous,
And that the lean abhorred monster keeps
Thee here in dark to be his paramour?

For fear of that, I still stay with thee:
And never from this palace of dim night
Depart again: here, here will I remain
With worms that are thy chamber-maids; O, here
Will I set up my everlasting rest,
And shake the yoke of inauspicious stars
From this world-wearied flesh. Eyes, look you last!
Arms, take your last embrace! and, lips, O you
The doors of breath, seal with a righteous kiss
A dateless bargain to engrossing death!
Come, bitter conduct, come unsavory guide!
Thou desperate pilot, now at once run on
The dashing rocks thy sea-sick weary bark!
Here's to my love! [*Drinks.*] O true apothecary!
Thy drugs are quick. Thus with a kiss I die. [*Dies.*]

HAMLET
LAERTES—ACT I, SCENE 3

AGE: Young   INTENT: Serious

L aertes' relationship with young Prince Hamlet before the events of
the play unfold has always been left to speculation. What is known
about Laertes is that he is devoted to his sister, Ophelia, and he is fond
of his long-winded father, Polonius.

Laertes has petitioned and gained permission from the new king of
Denmark, Claudius, to return to Paris. But before he departs, just as
his father gives him advice on how to behave in Paris, Laertes
admonishes his sister concerning her infatuation with Prince Hamlet.

LAERTES

My necessaries are embark'd: farewell:
And, sister, as the winds give benefit
And convoy is assistant, do not sleep,
But let me hear from you.
For Hamlet and the trifling of his favour,
Hold it in fashion and a toy in blood,

A violet in the youth of primy nature,
Forward, not permanent, sweet, not lasting,
The perfume and suppliance of a minute,
No more. Think it no more:
For nature, crescent, does not grow alone
In thews and bulk, but, as this temple waxes,
The inward service of the mind and soul
Grows wide withal. Perhaps he loves you now,
And now no soil nor cautel doth besmirch
The virtue of his will: but you must fear,
His greatness weigh'd, his will is not his own;
For he himself is subject to his birth:
He may not, as unvalu'd persons do,
Carve for himself; for on his choice depends
The safety and health of this whole state;
And therefore must his choice be circumscrib'd
Unto the voice and yielding of that body
Whereof he is the head. Then if he says he loves you,
It fits your wisdom so far to believe it
As he in his particular act and place
May give his saying deed; which is no further
Than the main voice of Denmark goes withal.
Then weigh what loss your honour may sustain,
If with too credent ear you list his songs,
Or lose your heart, or your chaste treasure open
To his unmaster'd importunity.
Fear it, Ophelia, fear it, my dear sister,
And keep you in the rear of your affection,
Out of the shot and danger of desire.
The chariest maid is prodigal enough,
If she unmask her beauty to the moon:
Virtue itself 'scapes not calumnious strokes:
The canker galls the infants of the spring,
Too oft before their buttons be disclos'd,
And in the morn and liquid dew of youth
Contagious blastments are most imminent.
Be wary then; best safety lies in fear:
Youth to itself rebels, though none else near.

ANTONY AND CLEOPATRA
CLEOPARTA—ACT V, SCENE 2

AGE: Mature [Any age]   INTENT: Serious

Cleoparta is inargubly the most complete woman Shakespeare created. *Antony and Cleopatra* is the only one of the late, great tragedies that is a love-tragedy. But unlike the earliest love-tragedy, *Romeo and Juliet*, neither Antony nor Cleoparta can claim immaturity and youth as reasons for their actions. They are both mature, experienced people who should know the power that sex and love can exhort. Shakespeare's Cleoparta exerts her will and wiles over men by being contrary, ever changing in moods, tempestuous, cunning, and, above all, passionate.

Anthony and Cleopatra have lost their war with Octavius Caesar. Antony lost not out of lesser strength of arms or men or ability as a general. He lost because he was so obsessed with Cleopatra that he followed her in flight from the great sea battle at Actium—a battle he might have well won.

Now, Antony is dead by his own hand; and Caesar is taking possession of Egypt. Left alone, Cleopatra awaits the arrival of Caesar and to carry out her plans for her own unique death in her "monument" (tomb). She is distraught, defeated, resigned to her plan. Her dreams and ambitions are dissolved. She, an absolute woman and queen, always the conqueror, must now be at the mercy of a conqueror. Into her presence comes Dolabella, a Roman who has known her and is now with Caesar. She does not recognize him in her distracted state, but she does ask him what is foremost on her mind: was there ever such an Antony as she imagined him to be?

CLEOPATRA

I dream'd there was an Emperor Antony:
O, such another sleep, that I might see
But such another man!
His face was as the heavens; and therein stuck
A sun and moon, which kept their course, and lighted
The little O, the earth.

His legs bestrid the ocean: his rear'd arm
Crested the world: his voice was propertied
As all the tuned spheres, and that to friends;
But when he meant to quail and shake the orb,
He was as rattling thunder. For his bounty,
There was no winter in't; and autumn 'twas
That grew the more by reaping: his delights
Were dolphin-like; they show'd his back above
The element they lived in; in his livery
Walk'd crowns and crownets; realms and islands were
As plates dropp'd from his pocket.
Think you there was, or might be, such a man
As this I dream'd of?
But, if there be, or ever were, one such,
It's past the size of dreaming: nature wants stuff
To vie strange forms with fancy; yet, to imagine
An Antony, were nature's piece 'gainst fancy,
Condemning shadows quite.

CORIOLANUS
VOLUMNIA—ACT V, SCENE 3

AGE: Mature   INTENT: Serious

Coriolanus is the last of the Roman plays, and it is almost entirely a
political play. Caius Marcius (later called Coriolanus") is a great
general and hero who has saved the Roman state and the Roman
people owe him much. He is persuaded to run for consul, but
Coriolanus is proud and haughty, with no love and only contempt for
the common people. He will not flatter them, and the people, in turn,
do not trust Coriolanus. He is not a good political candidate.

He loses the election as consul, and he is driven out of Rome and
into exile. He takes refuge with the Volscians, the enemy from whom
he had once saved Rome. Coriolanus leads the Volscians to victory
against Rome; he has Rome at his mercy. He is ready to burn Rome to
the ground. The Roman leaders, in a final act of desperation, persuade
Coriolanus' mother, Volumnia, to go to him and to plead for Rome.

Both the senators and Volumnia know she is the only one who might
be able to dissuade Coriolanus from his destructive intents. She must
save Rome.

Much has been made by many observers about the "beauty" of
Volumnia's character, and the "touching" relationship she and
Coriolanus have. Volumnia is, admittedly, one of the most memorable
women Shakespeare created. Volumnia is, however, a stern Roman
matron, full of class pride, contempt for the people, thirsty for power,
and in many ways as courageous as her son. She is also the one
responsible for installing these characteristics in her son.

Volumnia comes to her son at the Volscian camp. She is accompa-
nied both by Virgilia, Coriolanus' wife, and by Young Marcius, his
son. They are dressed "in mourning habits."

VOLUMNIA

You have said you will not grant us any thing:
For we have nothing else to ask, but that
Which you deny already: yet we will ask:
That, if you fail in our request, the blame
May hang upon your hardness: therefore hear us.
Should we be silent and not speak, our raiment
And state of bodies would bewray what life
We have led since thy exile. Think with thyself
How more unfortunate than all living women
Are we come hither: since that thy sight, which should
Make our eyes flow with joy, hearts dance with comforts,
Constrains them weep and shake with fear and sorrow;
Making the mother, wife and child to see
The son, the husband and the father tearing
His country's bowels out. And to poor we
Thine enmity's most capital: thou barr'st us
Our prayers to the gods, which is a comfort
That all but we can enjoy; for how can we,
Alas, how can we for our country pray,
Whereto we are bound, together with thy victory,
Whereto are we bound? alack, or we must lose
The country, our dear nurse, or else thy person,

Or comfort in the country. We must find
An evident calamity, though we had
Our wish, which side should win: for either thou
Must, as a foreign recreant, be led
With manacles through our streets, or else
Triumphantly tread on thy country's ruin,
And bear the palm for having bravely shed
Thy wife and children's blood. For myself, son,
I purpose not to wait on fortune till
These wars determine: if I cannot persuade thee
Rather to show a noble grace to both parts
Than seek the end of one, thou shalt no sooner
March to assult thy country than to tread—
Trust to't, thou shalt not—on thy mother's womb
That brought thee to this world.
              Nay, go not from us thus.
If it were so that our request did tend
To save the Romans, thereby to destroy
The Volsces whom you serve, you might condemn us,
As poisonous of your honour: no, our suit
Is, that you reconcile them: while the Volsces
May say 'This mercy we have show'd'; the Romans,
'This we received'; and each in either side
Give the all-hail to thee, and cry 'Be blest
For making up this peace!' Thou know'st, great son,
The end of war's uncertain, but this certain,
That, if thou conquer Rome, the benefit
Which thou shalt thereby reap is such a name,
Whose reputation will be dogg'd with curses;
Whose chronicle thus writ: 'The man was noble,
But with his last attempt he wiped it out;
Destroy'd his country, and his name remains
To the ensuing age abhorr'd.' Speak to me, son:
Thou has affected the fine strains of honour,
To imitate the graces of the gods;
To tear with thunder the wide cheeks o' the air,
And yet to charge thy sulphur with a bolt
That should but rive an oak. Why dost not speak?

Think'st thou it honourable for a noble man
Still to remember wrongs? Daughter, speak you:
He cares not for your weeping. Speak thou, boy:
Perhaps thy childishness will move him more
Than can our reasons. There's no man in the world
More bound to's mother; yet here he lets me prate
Like one i' the stocks. Thou has never in thy life
Show'd thy dear mother any courtesy,
When she, poor hen, fond of no second brood,
Has cluck'd thee to the wars and safely home,
Loaden with honour. Say my request's unjust,
And spurn me back: but if it be not so,
Thou art not honest; and the gods will plague thee,
That thou restrain'st from me the duty which
To a mother's part belongs. He turns away:
Down, ladies; let us shame him with our knees.
To his surname Coriolanus 'longs more pride
Than pity to our prayers. Down: an end;
This is the last: so we will home to Rome,
And die among our neighbors. Nay, behold's:
This boy, that cannot tell what he would have,
But kneels and holds up hands for fellowship,
Does reason our petition with more strength
Than thou hast to deny 't. Come, let us go:
This fellow had a Volscian to his mother;
His wife is in Corioli and his child
Like him by chance. Yet give us our dispatch:
I am hush'd until our city be afire,
And then I'll speak a little.

ORDER DIRECT

MONOLOGUES THEY HAVEN'T HEARD, Karshner. Modern speeches written in the language of today. $7.95.

MORE MONOLOGUES THEY HAVEN'T HEARD, Karshner. More exciting living-language speeches. $7.95.

SCENES THEY HAVEN'T SEEN, Karshner. Modern scenes for men and women. $7.95.

FOR WOMEN, MONOLOGUES THEY HAVEN'T HEARD, Pomerance. Contemporary speeches for actresses. $7.95

MONOLOGUES FOR KIDS, Roddy. 28 wonderful speeches for boys and girls. $7.95.

MORE MONOLOGUES for KIDS, Roddy. More great speeches for boys and girls. $7.95.

SCENES FOR KIDS, Roddy. 30 scenes for girls and boys. $7.95.

MONOLOGUES FOR TEENAGERS, Karshner. Contemporary teen speeches. $7.95.

SCENES FOR TEENAGERS, Karshner. Scenes for today's teen boys and girls. $7.95.

HIGH SCHOOL MONOLOGUES THEY HAVEN'T HEARD, Karshner. Contemporary speeches for high schoolers, $7.95.

DOWN HOME MONOLOGUES, Karshner. Speeches for men and women in the language of rural America. $7.95.

MONOLOGUES FROM THE CLASSICS, ed. Karshner. Speeches from Shakespeare, Marlowe and others. An excellent collection for men and women, $7.95.

SCENES FROM THE CLASSICS, ed. Maag. Scenes from Shakespeare and others. $7.95.

SHAKESPEARE'S MONOLOGUES THEY HAVEN'T HEARD, ed. Dotterer. Lesser known speeches from The Bard. $7.95.

MONOLOGUES FROM CHEKHOV, trans. Cartwright. Modern translations from Chekhov's major plays: *Cherry Orchard, Uncle Vanya, Three Sisters, The Sea Gull.* $7.95.

MONOLOGUES FROM GEORGE BERNARD SHAW, ed. Michaels. Great speeches for men and women from the works of G.B.S. $7.95.

MONOLOGUES FROM OSCAR WILDE, ed. Michaels. The best of Wilde's urbane, dramatic writing from his greatest plays. For men and women. $7.95.

WOMAN, Susan Pomerance. Monologues for actresses. $7.95.

WORKING CLASS MONOLOGUES, Karshner. Speeches from blue collar occupations. Waitress, cleaning lady, policewoman, truck driver, miner, etc. $7.95.

MODERN SCENES FOR WOMEN, Pomerance. Modern scenes for today's versatile actresses. $7.95.

MONOLOGUES FROM MOLIERE, trans. Dotterer. A definitive collection of speeches from the French Master. The first translation into English prose. $7.95.

SHAKESPEARE'S MONOLOGUES FOR WOMEN, trans. Dotterer. $7.95.

DIALECT MONOLOGUES, Karshner/Stern.13 essential dialects applied to contemporary monologues. Book and Cassette Tape. $19.95.

YOU SAID A MOUTHFUL, Karshner. Tongue twisters galore. Great exercises for actors, singers, public speakers. Fun for everyone. $7.95.

TEENAGE MOUTH, Karshner. Modern monologues for young men and women. $7.95.

SHAKESPEARE'S LADIES, Dotterer. A second book of Shakespeare's monologues for women. With a descriptive text on acting Shakespeare. $7.95.

BETH HENLEY:MONOLOGUES FOR WOMEN, Henley.*Crimes of the Heart* and others. $7.95.

CITY WOMEN, Smith. 20 powerful, urban monologues. Great audition pieces. $7.95.

KIDS' STUFF, Roddy. 30 great audition pieces for children. $7.95.

KNAVES, KNIGHTS, and **KINGS**, Dotterer. Speeches for men from Shakespeare. $8.95.

DIALECT MONOLOUES, VOL II, Karshner/Stern. 14 more important dialects. Farsi, Afrikaans, Asian Indian, etc. Book and Cassette tape. $19.95.

RED LICORICE, Tippit. 31 great scene-monologues for preteens. $7.95.

MODERN MONOLOGUES for MODERN KIDS, Mauro. $7.95.

Your check or money order (no cash or COD) plus handling charges of $2.50 for the first book, and $1.50 for each additional book. California residents add 8.25 % tax. Send your order to: Dramaline Publications, 36851 Palm View Road, Rancho Mirage, California 92270.